GABRIEL YARED

CW00530244

THE PIANO COLLECTION

PUBLISHED BY
WISE PUBLICATIONS
14-15 BERNERS STREET, LONDON,
W1T 3LJ, UK.

EXCLUSIVE DISTRIBUTORS:
MUSIC SALES LIMITED
DISTRIBUTION CENTRE, NEWMARKET ROAD,
BURY ST EDMUNDS, SUFFOLK,
IP33 3YB, UK.

MUSIC SALES PTY LIMITED
120 ROTHSCHILD AVENUE, ROSEBERY,
NSW 2018, AUSTRALIA.

ORDER NO. AM983697
ISBN 978-1-84609-223-7
THIS BOOK © COPYRIGHT 2007
WISE PUBLICATIONS, A DIVISION OF
MUSIC SALES LIMITED.

EDITED BY ANN BARKWAY
ARRANGED BY DEREK JONES.

PRINTED IN THE EU.

WWW.MUSICSALES.COM

WISE PUBLICATIONS
PART OF THE MUSIC SALES GROUP

LONDON / NEW YORK / PARIS / SYDNEY / COPENHAGEN / BERLIN / MADRID / TOKYO

£17.95

CHARLOTTE AND WILL

FROM 'AUTUMN IN NEW YORK' (2001)

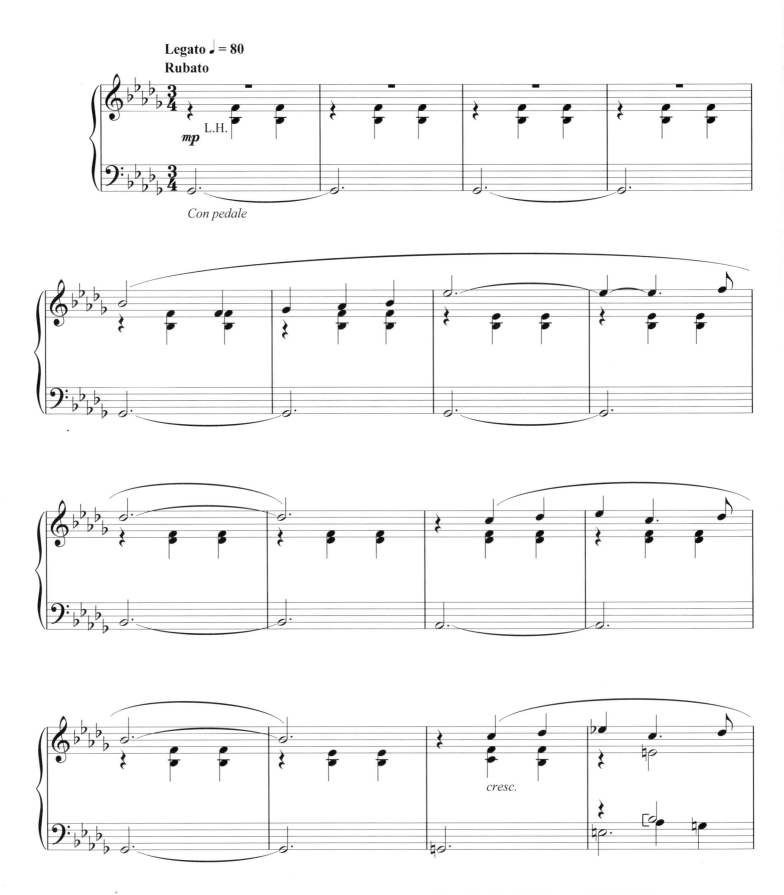

3

DES ORAGES POUR LA NUIT

FROM 'BETTY BLUE' (1986)

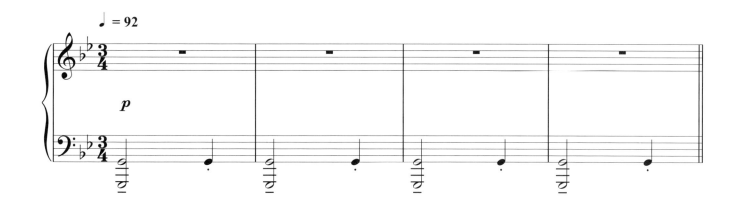

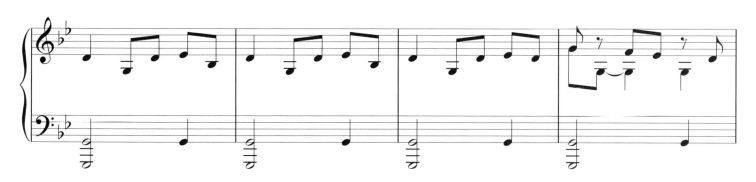

BETTY ET ZORG

FROM 'BETTY BLUE' (1986)

Slowly ♩ = 72

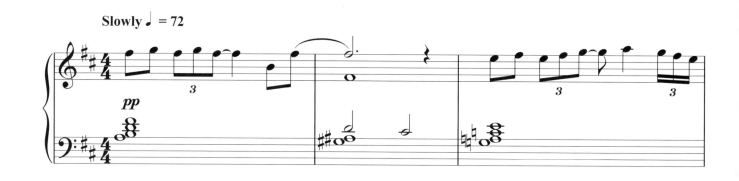

C'EST LE VENT BETTY

FROM 'BETTY BLUE' (1986)

Slowly ♩ = 70

11

THE UNFEELING KISS

FROM 'CITY OF ANGELS' (1998)

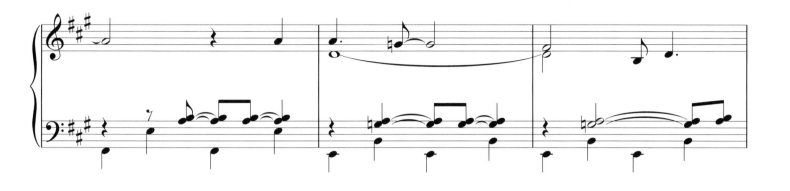

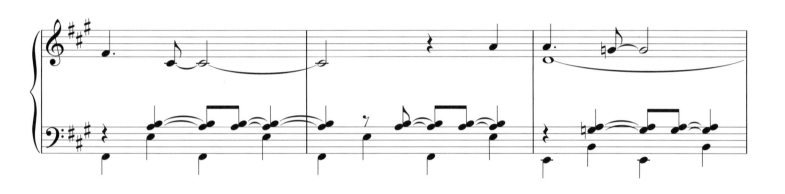

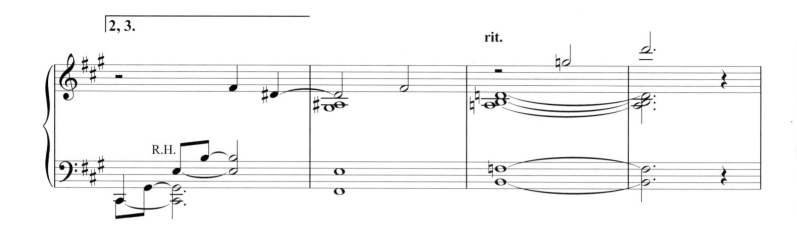

NOT TALKING

FROM 'BREAKING AND ENTERING' (2006)

MUSIC BY GABRIEL YARED, KARL HYDE AND RICHARD SMITH

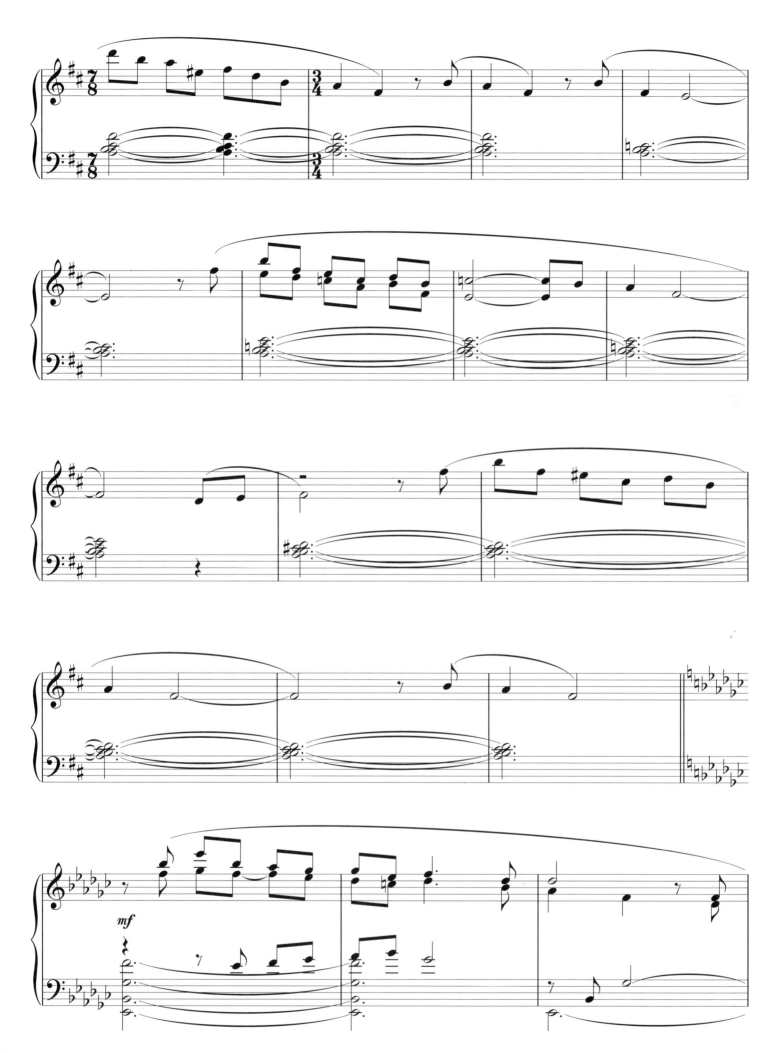

WILL AND AMIRA

FROM 'BREAKING AND ENTERING' (2006)

MUSIC BY GABRIEL YARED, KARL HYDE AND RICHARD SMITH

19

CAMILLE

FROM 'CAMILLE CLAUDEL' (1988)

ADA PLAYS TO INMAN

FROM 'COLD MOUNTAIN' (2003)

Gently ♩ = 120

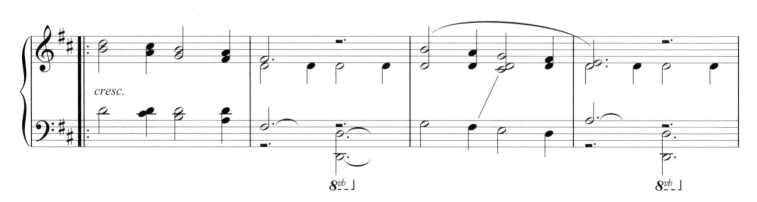

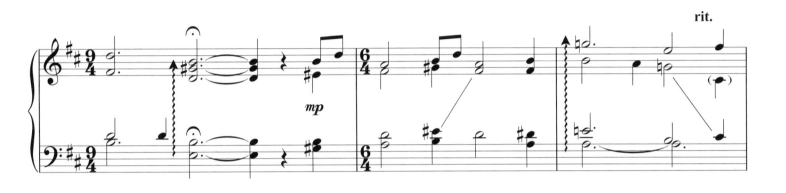

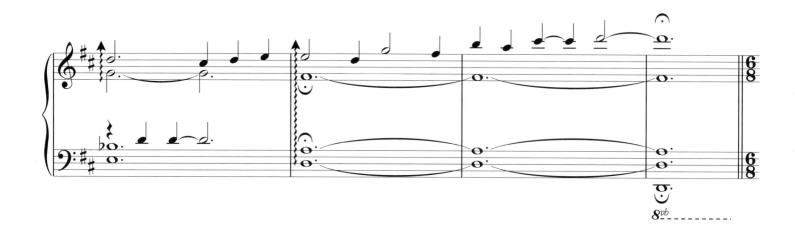

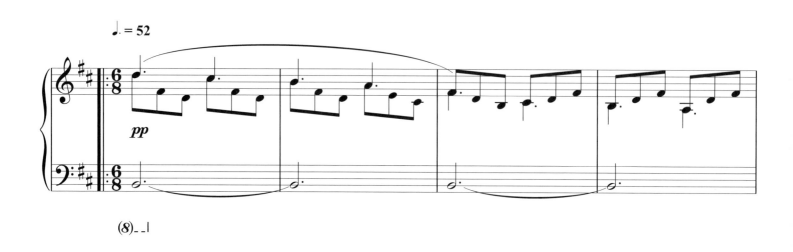

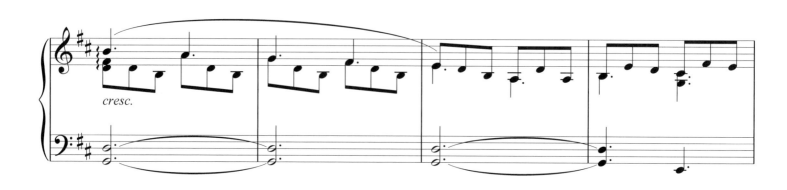

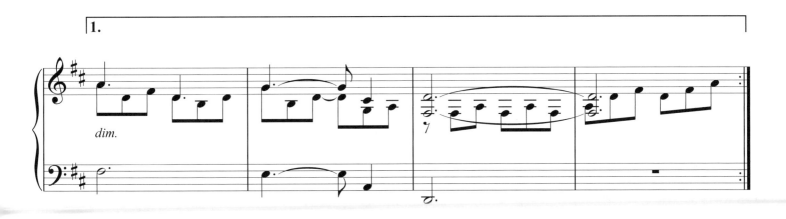

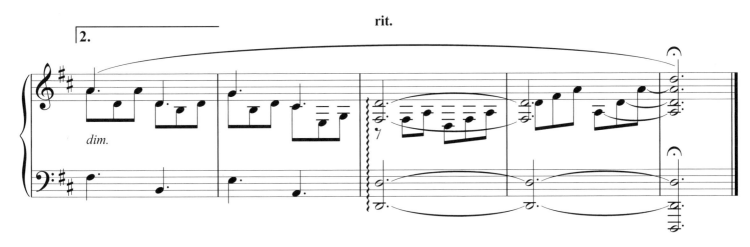

MONROE'S DEATH

FROM 'COLD MOUNTAIN' (2003)

DIE SONATE VOM GUTEN MENSCHEN

FROM 'THE LIVES OF OTHERS' ('DAS LEBEN DER ANDEREN') (2006)

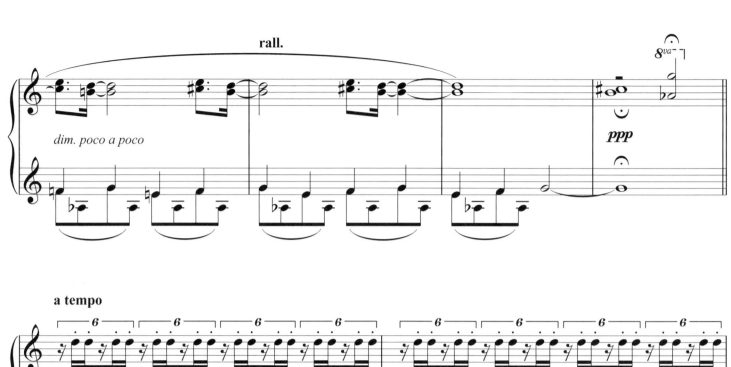

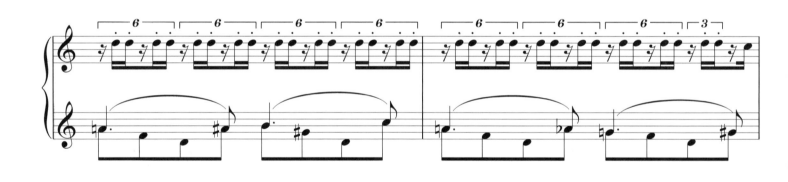

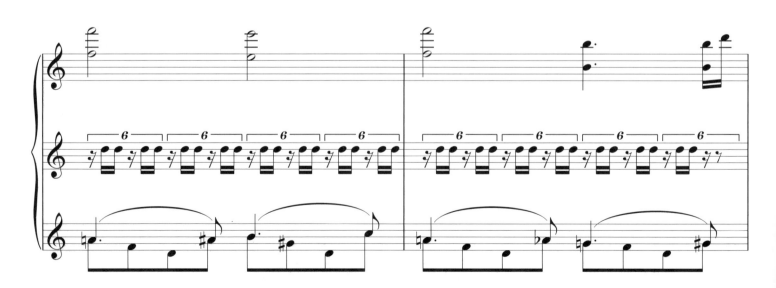

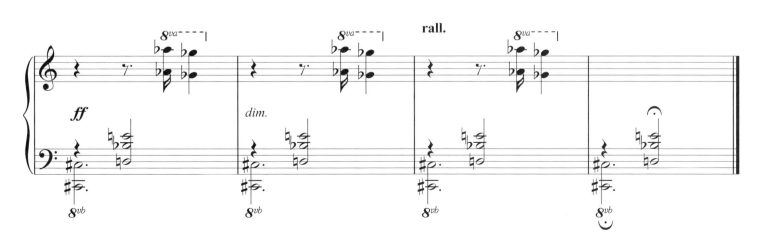

LIKE A BIRD

FROM 'MAP OF THE HUMAN HEART' (1993)

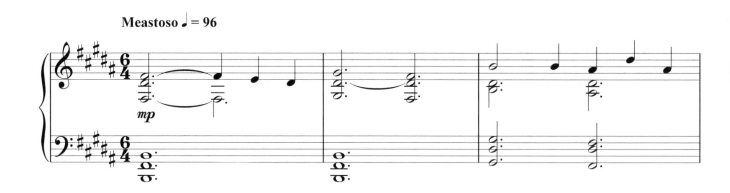

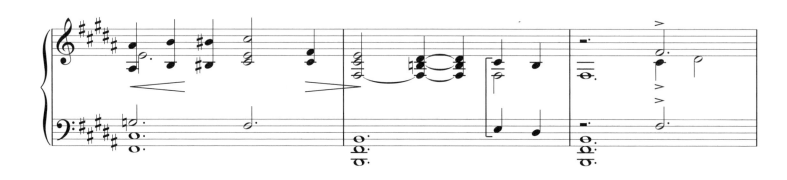

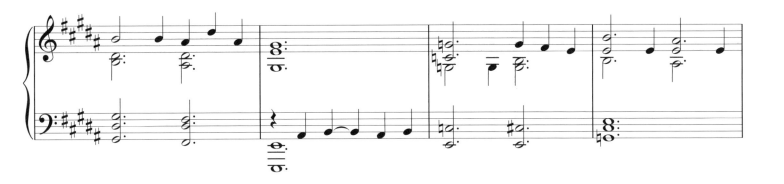

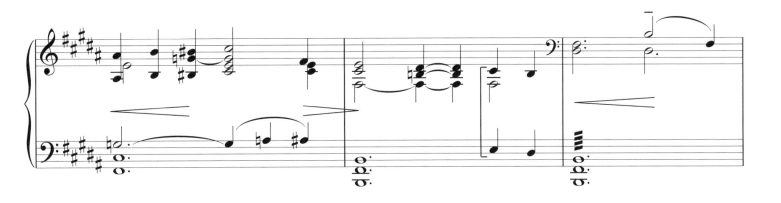

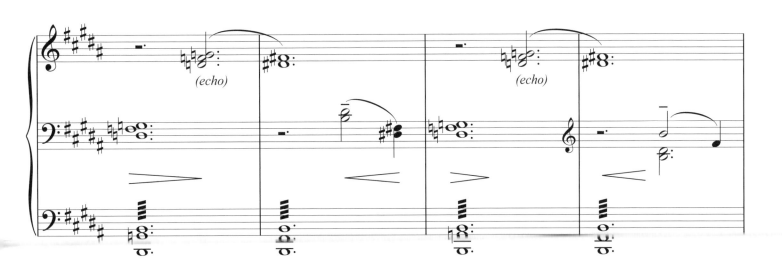

LOVERS ON BALLOON

FROM 'MAP OF THE HUMAN HEART' (1993)

LE PIANO (WALTZ IN C)

FROM 'L'AVION' (2005)

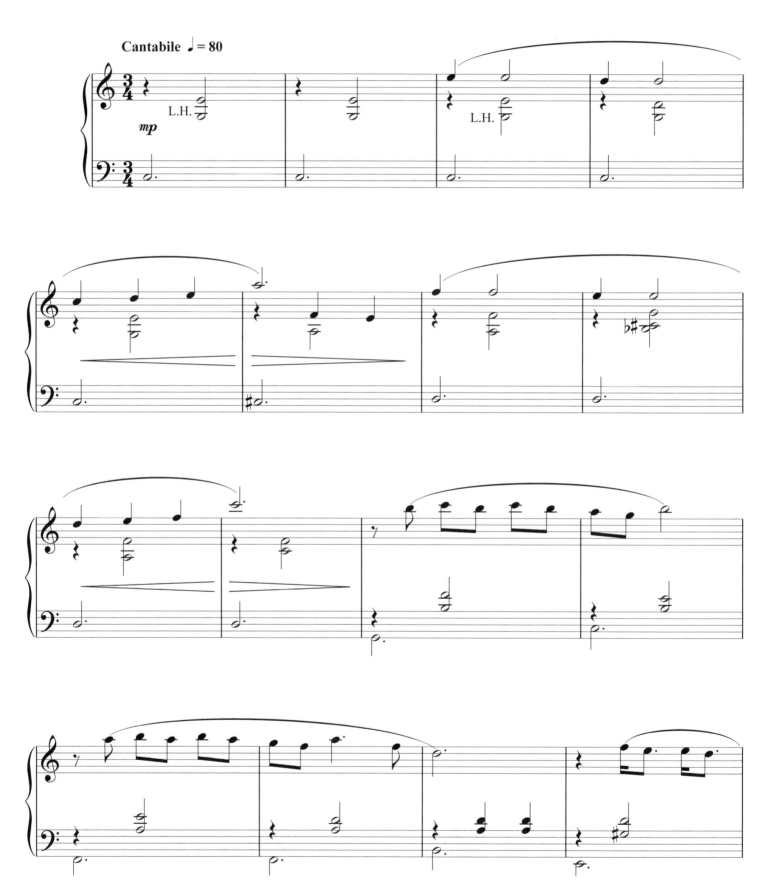

43

L'AMANT

MAIN THEME FROM 'THE LOVER' ('L'AMANT') (1992)

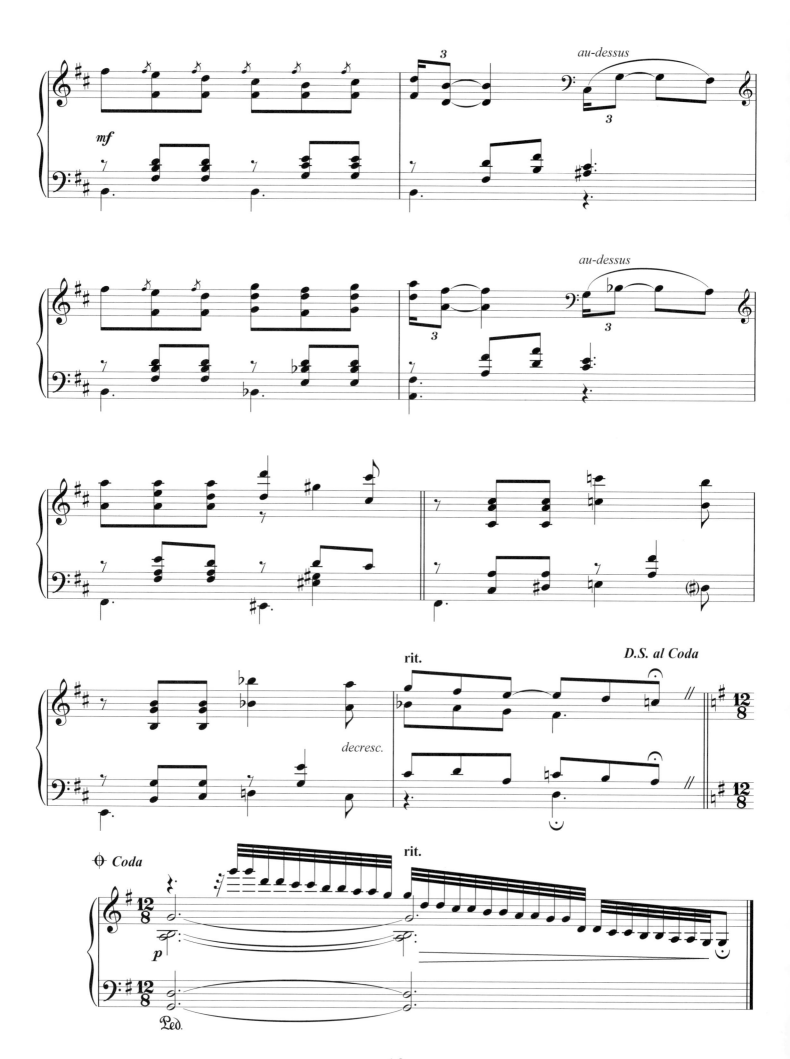

NOCTURNE

FROM 'THE LOVER' ('L'AMANT') (1992)

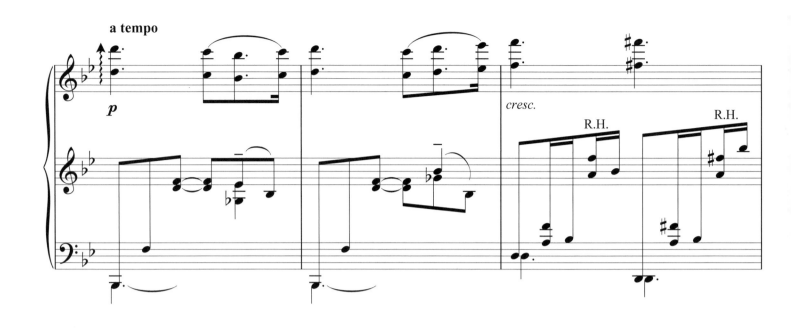

poco rit.　a tempo

52

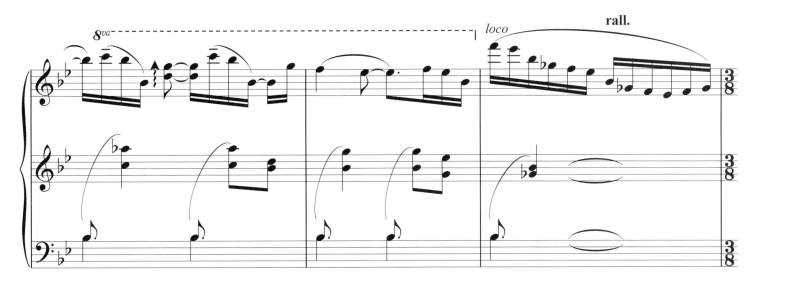

POSSESSO

FROM 'POSSESSION' (2002)

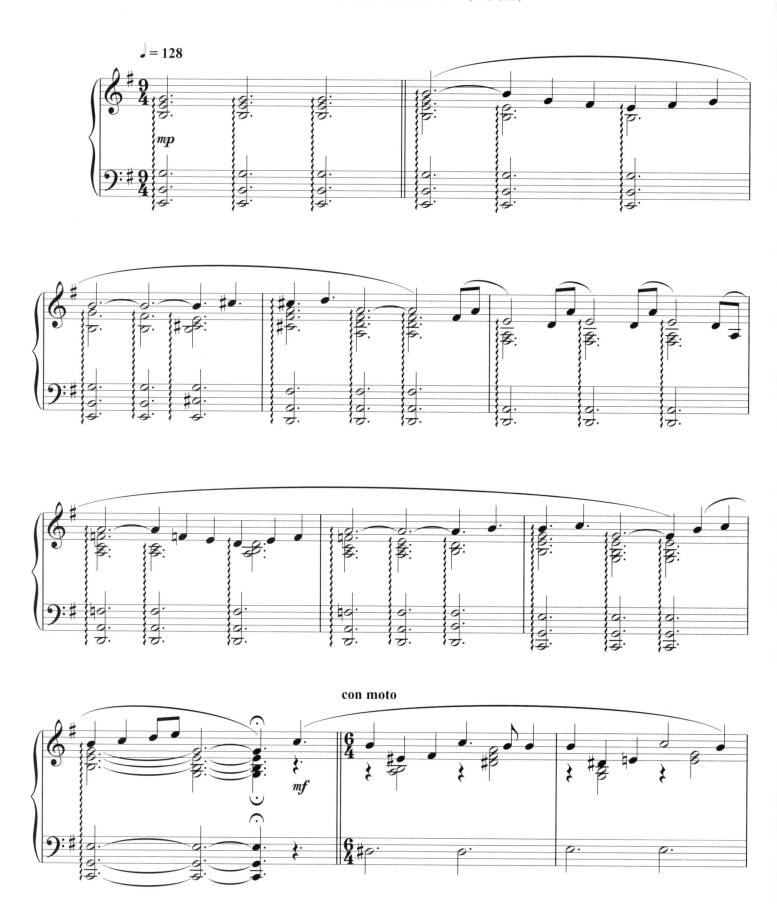

poco rit.

a tempo

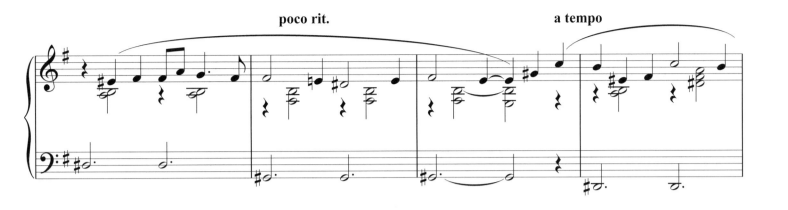

rit.

mp

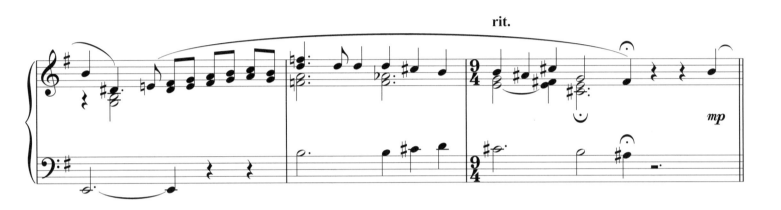

a tempo

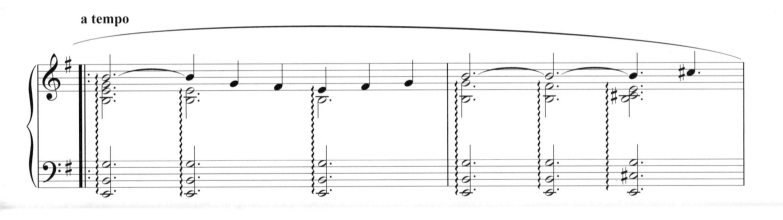

meno mosso

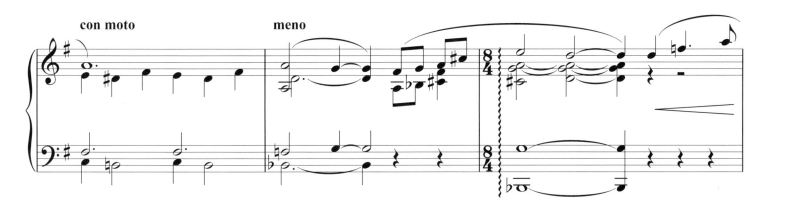

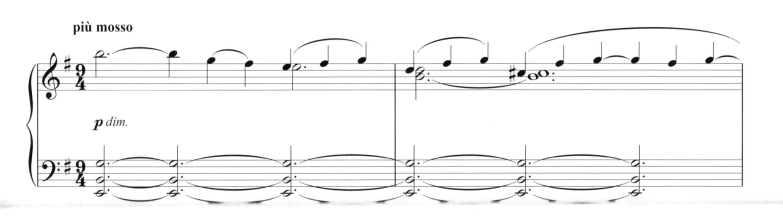

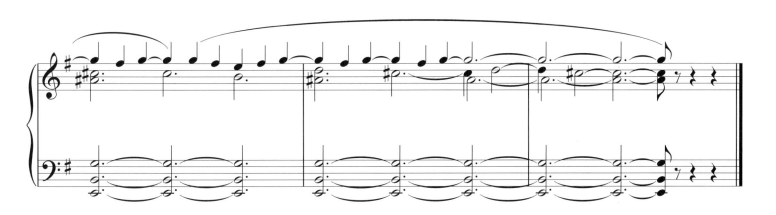

LULLABY FOR CAÏN

FROM 'THE TALENTED MR RIPLEY' (1999)

MAIN THEME

FROM 'THE TALENTED MR RIPLEY' (1999)

To Coda ⊕

63

L'IMAGINAIRE

FROM 'SAUVE QUI PEUT LA VIE' (1980)

Slowly and freely

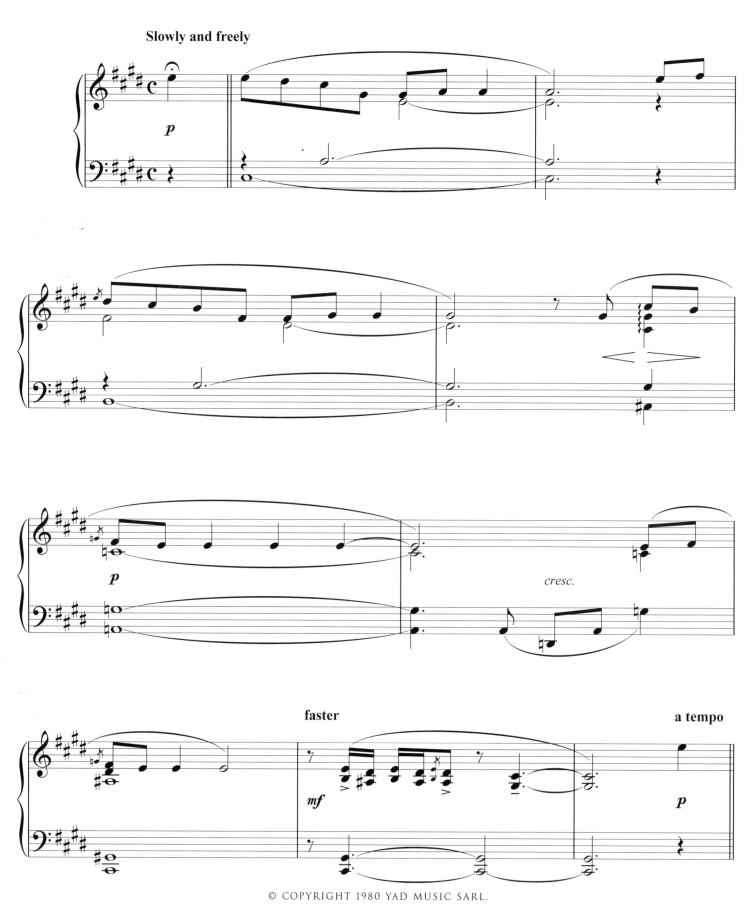

SYLVIA AND TED

FROM 'SYLVIA' (2003)

ROMANCE

FROM 'SYLVIA' (2003)

MAIN THEME

FROM 'THE ENGLISH PATIENT' (1996)

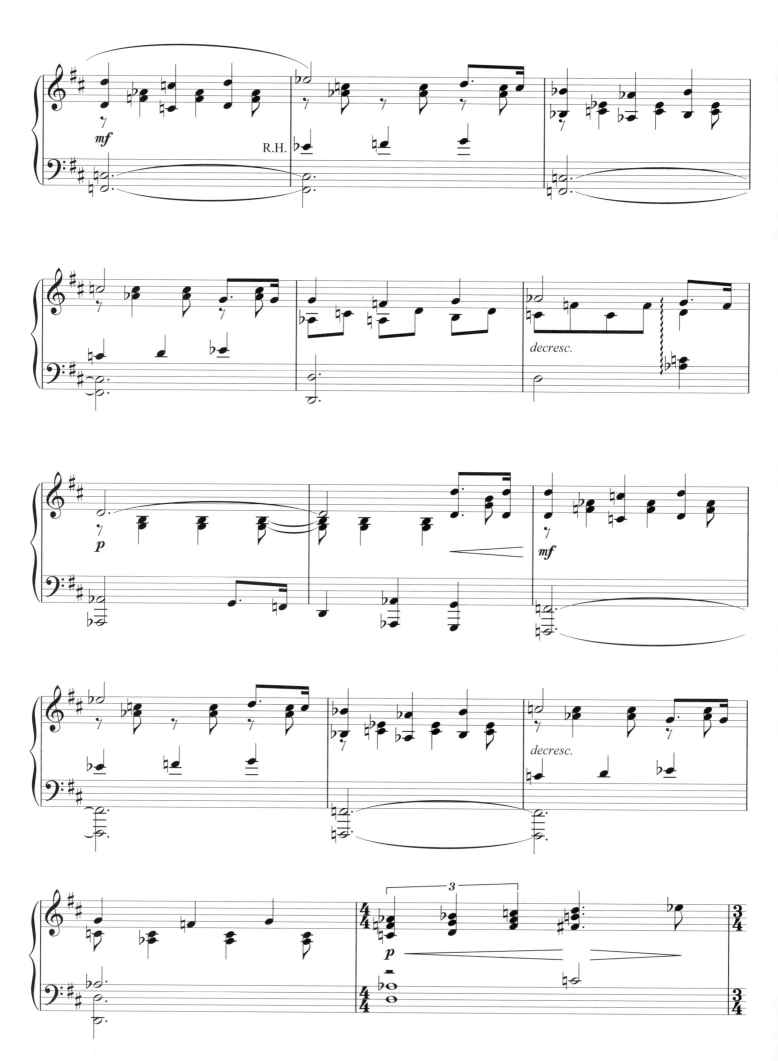

73

CONVENTO DI SANT'ANNA

FROM 'THE ENGLISH PATIENT' (1996)

rit.　　　　　　　　　　　　　　　　　　　　　　　　　　　piùlento

76

123456789